Practise Your Spelling Skills

THIRD EDITION

1

Carmel Perrett and John Rose

Pearson Australia
(a division of Pearson Australia Group Pty Ltd)
707 Collins Street, Melbourne, Victoria 3008
PO Box 23360, Melbourne, Victoria 8012
www.pearson.com.au

Copyright © Pearson Australia 2006
(a division of Pearson Australia Group Pty Ltd)
First published 2006 by Pearson Australia
Reprinted 2007 (three times), 2009, 2011, 2012, 2016

Edited by Anne McKenna
Cover and interior design by Kim Ferguson
Illustrations by Christina Miesen
Cover image by Getty Images
Prepress work by The Type Factory
Produced by Pearson Australia
Printed in Australia by the SOS Print + Media Group

ISBN 978-0-7339-7494-6

Pearson Australia Group Pty Ltd   ABN 40 004 245 943

Contents

Spelling and writing

This spelling program has been prepared in response to a defined need. Spelling is one of the sub-skills of writing, along with appropriate syntactical structures, punctuation, vocabulary development and handwriting. Writing activities in the primary school should, wherever possible, emphasise the interrelatedness of these sub-skills as well as of the other areas of language – listening, speaking and reading.

For written communication children need to have the desire and ability to express themselves through writing their ideas, thoughts, feelings and knowledge with increasing confidence and skill.

Spelling ability grows most effectively when viewed as an integral part of the total language program, and is developed through a continuous program that recognises both increasing ability and changing interests of the writer. As children develop the desire to communicate their ideas in writing, they need skills in spelling that can be provided systematically. The skills and the appropriate experiences can, in many instances, go hand in hand.

In this book ...

This book contains 40 units. Four are revision units based on seasonal themes.

The first unit revises the single sounds that most children would have covered in the preparatory year at school. The next units cover three-letter words, followed in a natural progression by more difficult word groupings. In addition there are five theme word groupings on numbers, families, pets, days and colours interspersed throughout the book. Units 38 and 39 look at essential words. These high-frequency words, along with some words already included in previous units, make up approximately half the vocabulary children use in their everyday reading, writing, speaking and listening.

Overall, the book is sequential in nature and provides a comprehensive cover of the spelling requirements for these young children through cloze activities, as well as open-ended activities, to stimulate imaginative thinking.

For teacher use, dictation sentences have been provided at the end of the book. They have been designed so that each one include words from a particular unit as well as words children have come across in previous units, which provides a built-in revision process. There is also a suggested list of blends and a record sheet. Teachers will no doubt also be using additional thematic words, according to what is of current interest in the classroom, to supplement the list words in this resource book. Room for children to list spelling words from these or other activities is provided on pages 88 to 91.

Features of this book

Focus letter

Word list (3-letter words) with focus letter highlighted

Word list for Theme unit

Word list for Revision unit

Word list for Essential words unit

Activities in which children explore and practise the word list words

Open-ended activity

Activities in which children explore and practise the word list words

Open-ended activity

Activities in which children explore words and apply knowledge of words from earlier units

Open-ended activity

Activities in which children explore and practise their frequently used words

Open-ended activity

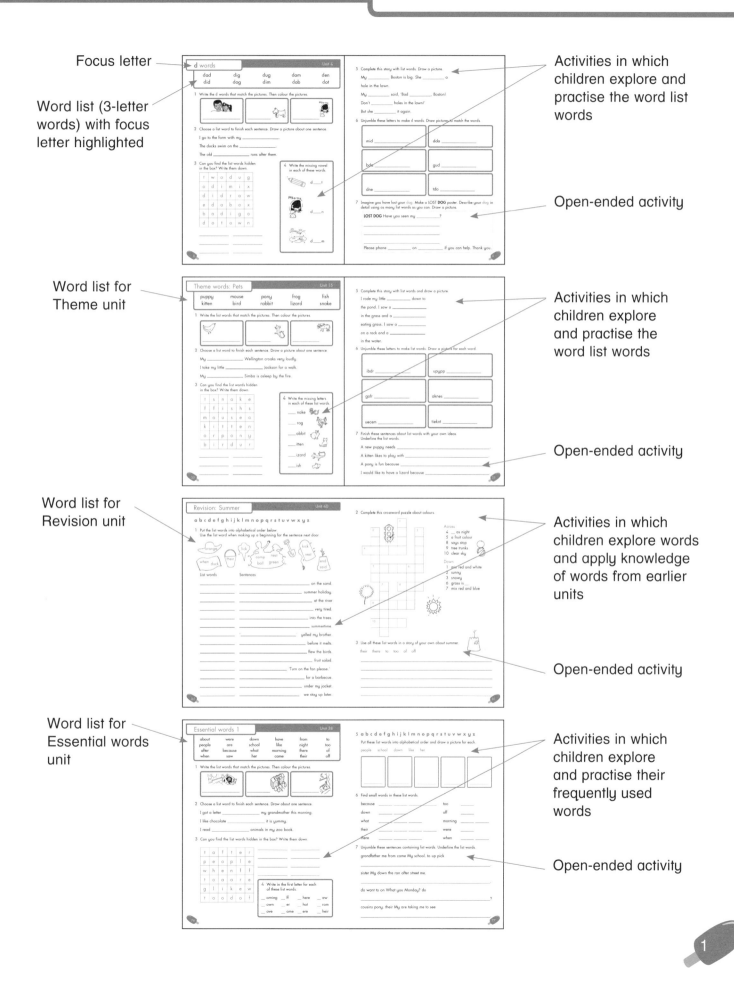

Revision of single sounds

Write the initial letter
of each word and colour
the picture.

b words

bad	bat	big	box	bus
bag	bed	bit	bun	but

1 Write the **b** words that match the pictures. Then colour the pictures.

_____

_____

_____

2 Choose a list word to finish each sentence. Draw a picture about one sentence.

Sally likes to go on the _____.

We look in the _____ pet shop.

The pups sleep in a _____.

3 Can you find the list words hidden in the box? Write them down. The first one is done for you.

m	e	n	b	i	t
b	u	t	h	e	n
c	s	b	a	d	d
s	o	b	e	d	s
c	b	o	x	e	s
b	i	g	t	i	n

__bit_____   _____

_____   _____

_____   _____

4 Write the missing vowel in each of these words.

b ____ s

b ____ t

b ____ d

b ____ g

b ____ x

4

5 Find and write list words to answer 'What am I?'

I have wheels.   I can fly.   I help carry things.
I go on the road.   I have fur.   I have handles.

What am I?   What am I?   What am I?

_____   _____   _____

6 Unjumble these letters to make **b** words. Draw pictures to match the words.

xbo _____   dab _____

bsu _____   bta _____

nub _____   gbi _____

7 Use these list words in sentences of your own.

box _____

but _____

big _____

bun _____

5

c words

can	**c**at	**c**up	**c**ab
cap	**c**ot	**c**ut	**c**ub

1 Write the **c** words that match the pictures. Then colour the pictures.

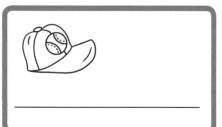

_____

_____

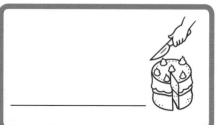

_____

2 Choose a list word to finish each sentence. Draw a picture about one sentence.

Matthew is a _____ scout.

He wears a _____.

He _____ go camping.

3 Can you find the list words hidden in the box? Write them down.

m	u	d	c	o	t
c	a	n	e	a	r
c	a	c	a	b	r
c	u	b	m	o	p
a	b	c	c	u	p
d	e	c	a	t	f

_____ _____

_____ _____

_____ _____

4 Write the missing vowel in each of these words.

c ____ t

c ____ n

c ____ t

c ____ p

c ____ b

6

5 Find list words to match these patterns.

6 Find and write a list word to go with each of these words. Draw a picture for each.

taxi _____

watering _____

lion _____

school _____

pussy _____

tea _____

7 Write a story about a cat. Use as many of the list words as you can.

_____

_____

_____

_____

d words

dad	**d**ig	**d**ug	**d**am	**d**en
did	**d**og	**d**im	**d**ab	**d**ot

1 Write the **d** words that match the pictures. Then colour the pictures.

_____ _____ _____

2 Choose a list word to finish each sentence. Draw a picture about one sentence.

I go to the farm with my _____.

The ducks swim on the _____.

The old _____ runs after them.

3 Can you find the list words hidden in the box? Write them down.

t	w	o	d	u	g
o	d	i	m	i	x
d	i	d	r	a	w
e	d	a	b	o	x
b	a	d	i	g	o
d	o	t	o	w	n

_____ _____

_____ _____

_____ _____

4 Write the missing vowel in each of these words.

d____t

d____n

d____m

8

5 Complete this story with list words. Draw a picture.

My _____ Boston is big. She _____ a

hole in the lawn.

My _____ said, 'Bad _____, Boston!

Don't _____ holes in the lawn!'

But she _____ it again.

6 Unjumble these letters to make **d** words. Draw pictures to match the words.

mid _____

dda _____

bda _____

gud _____

dne _____

tdo _____

7 Imagine you have lost your dog. Make a LOST DOG poster. Describe your dog in detail using as many list words as you can. Draw a picture.

LOST DOG Have you seen my _____?

_____

_____

_____

Please phone _____ on _____ if you can help. Thank you.

Theme words: Numbers

one	three	five	seven	nine
two	four	six	eight	ten

1 Write the list words that match the pictures. Then colour the pictures.

_____

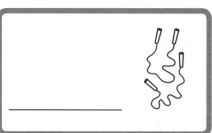

_____

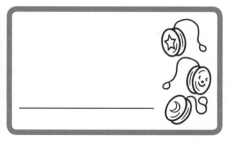

_____

2 Choose a list word to finish each sentence. Draw a picture about one sentence.

A dog has _____ legs.

A pig has _____ears.

An octopus has _____ legs.

3 Can you find the list words hidden in the box? Write them down.

a	m	t	e	n	t
f	i	v	e	m	s
s	e	v	e	n	o
n	o	n	e	z	a
o	r	s	i	x	j
e	n	f	o	u	r

_____   _____

_____   _____

_____   _____

4 Write the missing letters in each of these words.

nin ____   ••••• / •••••• (dots)

eig ____ ____   •••• / ••••

thr ____ ____   •••

sev ____ ____   ••• / ••••

fou ____   ••••

fiv ____   •••••

5 Complete this rhyme with list words and draw a picture.

One, _____, buckle my shoe.

Three,_____, knock at the door.

Five, _____, pick up sticks.

Seven, _____, lay them straight.

Nine, _____, a big, fat hen.

6 Unjumble these letters to make number words. Draw pictures to match the words.

owt _____

vief _____

etigh _____

net _____

einn _____

oruf _____

7 Finish these sentences containing list words with your own ideas. Underline the list words.

When I was one I could _____.

When I was three I could _____.

When I was five I could _____.

When I am ten I want to _____.

f words

fat	fix	fun	fig	fit
fed	fox	fan	fin	fog

1 Write the **f** words that match the pictures. Then colour the pictures.

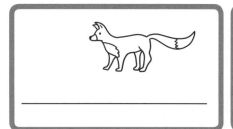  

_____ _____ _____

2 Choose a list word to finish each sentence. Draw a picture about one sentence.

We had _____ at the farm.

I _____ the pigs.

They were very _____.

3 Can you find the list words hidden in the box? Write them down.

f	i	x	a	r	t
l	o	a	f	i	t
s	f	e	d	o	g
s	u	r	f	u	n
k	f	i	g	o	t
f	i	n	i	n	e

_____ _____

_____ _____

_____ _____

4 Write the missing vowel in each of these words.

f____n

f____n

f____g

5 Find list words to match these patterns.

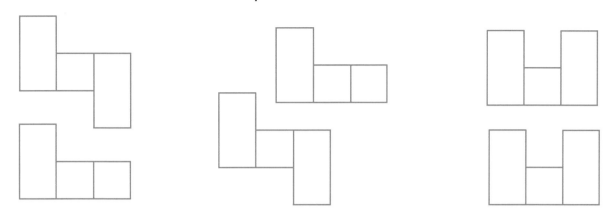

6 Unjumble these letters to make **f** words. Draw pictures to match the words.

nfa _____

fnu _____

gif _____

xfo _____

gof _____

taf _____

7 Find a list word to match each clue.

a wild animal with a long bushy tail _____

thick mist _____

not thin _____

part of a fish's body _____

g words

get	gum	gap	gas
got	gun	god	gut

1 Write the **g** words that match the pictures. Then colour the pictures.

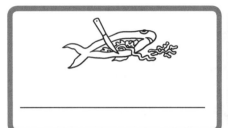

_____

_____

_____ boots

2 Choose a list word to finish each sentence. Draw a picture about one sentence.

We _____ up at six o'clock and go fishing.

We wear _____ boots.

I can _____ the fish.

3 Can you find the list words hidden in the box? Write them down.

c	a	r	g	a	p
a	g	e	t	l	p
t	e	r	g	o	d
g	o	t	e	n	t
m	u	d	g	a	s
s	g	u	t	w	o

_____ _____

_____ _____

_____ _____

4 Write the missing vowel in each of these words.

g____n

g____s

g____m boots

14

5 Find list words to match these patterns.

6 Unjumble these letters to make **g** words. Draw pictures to match the words.

pag _____

ugn _____

sag _____

tge _____

tgu _____

tog _____

7 Use the list words got and get when completing these sentences.

For my last birthday I _____

_____.

For my next birthday I want to _____

_____.

15

has	**h**en	**h**it	**h**is	**h**ot
hat	**h**id	**h**im	**h**op	**h**ut

1 Write the **h** words that match the pictures. Then colour the pictures.

_____

_____

_____

2 Choose a list word to finish each sentence. Draw a picture about one sentence.

Michelle likes to swim on _____ days.

She _____ a lot of fun.

Her sun _____ is pink.

3 Can you find the list words hidden in the box? Write them down.

a	n	t	h	i	t
p	h	i	s	e	r
s	l	h	o	p	e
h	a	s	m	a	n
c	e	h	i	d	k
i	h	i	m	l	i

_____ _____

_____ _____

_____ _____

4 Write the missing vowel in each of these words.

    h____p

    h____n

    h____t

5 Find list words to match these patterns.

6 Complete these crossword puzzles with list words.

A   B   C   D

A Across something you wear on your head
Down owns something

B Across that man
Down very sunny

C Across to move on one leg
Down an animal that lays eggs

D Across you do this with a bat and ball
Down belongs to him

7 Write a story about a hen. Use as many of the list words as you can.

_____

_____

_____

_____

17

Theme words: Family

mother	grandmother	cousin	brother	uncle
sister	aunt	father	grandfather	baby

1 Write the list words that match the pictures. Then colour the pictures.

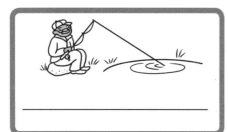

_____

_____

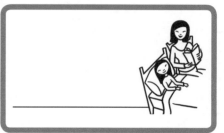

_____

2 Choose a list word to finish each sentence. Draw a picture about one sentence.

My _____ Henry works on a farm.

My _____ Monica has a red car.

My _____ Rachel is in Grade 6.

3 Can you find the list words hidden in the box? Write them down.

t	m	b	a	b	y	g
f	a	u	n	t	w	v
s	i	s	t	e	r	o
u	n	c	l	e	a	l
c	o	u	s	i	n	t
e	f	a	t	h	e	r

_____   _____

_____   _____

_____   _____

4 Write the missing letters in each of these list words.

broth ____ ____

grandmoth ____ ____

sist ____ ____

fath ____ ____

moth ____ ____

grandfath ____ ____

5 Find and write list words to answer 'Who am I?'

I am young.
I live with your aunt.

Who am I?

I am little.
Sometimes I cry.

Who am I?

I am a boy.
Your Mum is mine too.

Who am I?

_____ _____ _____

6 Unjumble these letters to make list words. Draw pictures to match the words.

clneu _____

gahardfnter _____

ergrnadomht _____

rbeorth _____

oethmr _____

irtsse _____

7 Finish these sentences containing list words with your own ideas.
Underline the list words.

A baby can _____.

My mother sometimes _____.

My grandmother is _____.

My brother likes _____.

Revision: Autumn

a b c d e f g h i j k l m n o p q r s t u v w x y z

1 Put the list words from the leaves into alphabetical order below. Use the list word when making up a beginning for the sentence next door.

grandfather

two

dog

uncle

big

eight

has

fox

one

cat

List words   **Sentences**

_____   _____ to the zoo.

_____   _____ seven years old.

_____   _____ chases the ball.

_____   _____ on that truck.

_____   _____ across the paddock.

_____   _____ stay with us.

_____   _____ lots of leaves.

_____   _____ out in the bush.

_____   _____ on the apple tree.

_____   _____ took the children fishing.

2 Write these list words in rhyming groups.

_____   _____

_____   _____

cot   cut   got   gut

_____   _____

hut   but   hot   dot

3 Complete this crossword puzzle about families.

Across
1 my father's mother
3 my father's father
6 a very young child
7 I am her child.
8 my father's daughter
9 my cousin's father

Down
2 my mother's sister
4 I am his child.
5 my aunt's son
6 my mother's son

4 Use all these list words in a story of your own about autumn.

fed   hen   dog   dad   fun   but

_____

_____

_____

_____

j words

| jam | jig | jog | jab |
| jug | job | jet | jot |

1 Write the **j** words that match the pictures. Then colour the pictures.

 _____

 _____

 _____

2 Choose a list word to finish each sentence. Draw a picture about one sentence.

I like _____ tarts.

We saw the _____ in the sky.

My _____ is to set the table.

3 Can you find the list words hidden in the box? Write them down.

m	a	j	o	t	c
s	j	e	t	r	a
j	a	m	o	w	l
s	o	j	o	b	m
j	a	b	e	t	e
p	r	j	u	g	n

_____ _____

_____ _____

_____ _____

4 Write the missing vowel in each of these words.

j___m

j___g

j___t

22

5 What job do you have in your classroom? What job would you like to have? Write a letter to your teacher about it.

Dear _____,

I would like the _____ of _____.

because I _____

_____.

Thank you. From _____

6 Unjumble these letters to make j words. Draw pictures to match the words.

mja _____

jba _____

jgo _____

toj _____

tje _____

bjo _____

7 Find a list word to match each clue.

a type of aeroplane _____

something to put milk in _____

a sweet food often put on toast _____

to run slowly _____

23

l words

leg	lit	lot	lip	lad
let	log	lid	led	lap

1 Write the l words that match the pictures. Then colour the pictures.

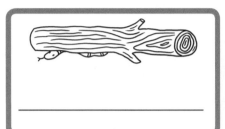
_____

_____

_____

2 Choose a list word to finish each sentence. Draw a picture about one sentence.

Please _____ me stay up late.

He was a _____ of help.

Put the _____ on the box.

3 Can you find the list words hidden in the box? Write them down.

s	l	e	d	o	n
l	a	d	y	e	s
s	l	a	p	e	n
p	i	c	l	o	t
e	s	l	i	t	m
c	u	p	l	e	t

_____ _____

_____ _____

_____ _____

4 Write the missing vowel in each of these words.

l____g

l____d

l____p

l____g

l____d

24

5 Find list words to match these patterns.

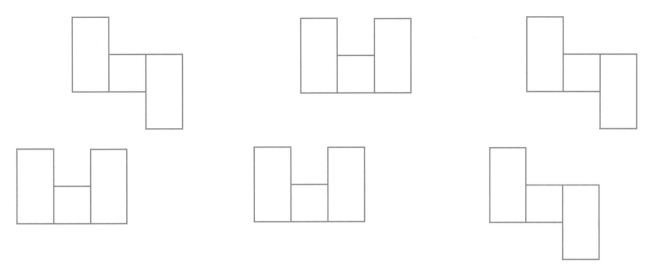

6 Complete these crossword puzzles with list words.

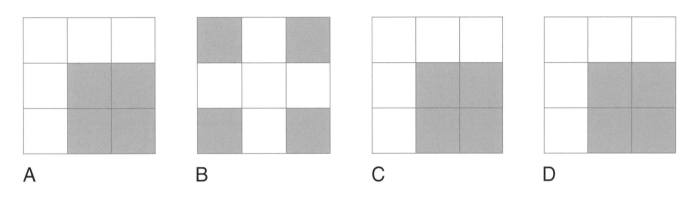

A   B   C   D

A   Across wood
      Down bright

B   Across teenage boy
      Down once around

C   Across part of the mouth
      Down walked my dog

D   Across the top of a box
      Down used for walking

7 Use these list words in sentences of your own.

lip _____

led _____

leg _____

log _____

m words

man	**m**en	**m**ud	**m**ap	**m**ug
mat	**m**et	**m**op	**m**ix	**m**um

1 Write the **m** words that match the pictures. Then colour the pictures.

_____

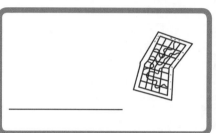
_____

_____

2 Choose a list word to finish each sentence. Draw a picture about one sentence.

That _____ is my dad.

I like to _____ the cake.

My cat likes to sit on the _____.

3 Can you find the list words hidden in the box? Write them down.

m	e	t	e	a	r
s	l	y	m	u	g
t	o	m	a	p	e
s	m	u	d	o	t
m	u	m	u	s	t
c	r	y	m	i	x

_____ _____

_____ _____

_____ _____

4 Write the missing vowel in each of these words.

m ____ n

m ____ p

m ____ g

m ____ t

m ____ p

26

5 Find and write list words for answers to 'What am I?'

I am sloppy.   I have roads.   Add this and that.
Pigs like me.   You read me.   Stir with a spoon.

What am I?   What am I?   What am I?

_____   _____   _____

6 Unjumble these letters to make **m** words. Draw pictures to match the words.

xmi _____

mgu _____

mmu _____

udm _____

nma _____

enm _____

7 Write a story about your mum, using as many of the list words as you can.

_____

_____

_____

_____

n words

net	nut	nip	nag
not	nap	nod	nun

1 Write the **n** words that match the pictures. Then colour the pictures.

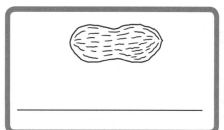

_____

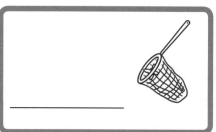

_____

_____

2 Choose a list word to finish each sentence. Draw a picture about one sentence.

The baby had a _____ in his cot.

A _____ means yes.

I did _____ get a letter.

3 Can you find the list words hidden in the box? Write them down.

p	n	o	t	e	n
s	n	a	g	d	e
n	a	p	e	n	t
s	o	n	o	d	e
w	n	u	n	e	t
i	t	s	n	i	p

_____ _____

_____ _____

_____ _____

4 Write the missing vowel in each of these words.

n____t

n____t

n____n

28

5 Find list words to rhyme with these words.

hot _____   bet _____   fun _____   cut _____

lap _____   bag _____   rod _____   pip _____

pot _____   pet _____   rag _____   tip _____

pod _____   hut _____   tap _____   sun _____

6 Unjumble these letters to make **n** words. Draw pictures to match the words.

ang _____

etn _____

tnu _____

pni _____

nnu _____

otn _____

7 Use these list words in sentences of your own.

nip _____

nag _____

net _____

not _____

Theme words: Pets

puppy	mouse	pony	frog	fish
kitten	bird	rabbit	lizard	snake

1 Write the list words that match the pictures. Then colour the pictures.

_____

_____

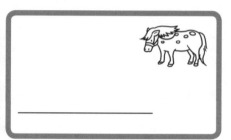

_____

2 Choose a list word to finish each sentence. Draw a picture about one sentence.

My _____ Wellington croaks very loudly.

I take my little _____ Jackson for a walk.

My _____ Simba is asleep by the fire.

3 Can you find the list words hidden in the box? Write them down.

t	s	n	a	k	e
f	f	i	s	h	s
m	o	u	s	e	o
k	i	t	t	e	n
o	r	p	o	n	y
b	i	r	d	u	r

_____   _____

_____   _____

_____   _____

4 Write the missing letters in each of these list words.

____ nake

____ rog

____ abbit

____ itten

____ izard

____ ish

30

5 Complete this story with list words and draw a picture.

I rode my little _____ down to

the pond. I saw a _____

in the grass and a _____

eating grass. I saw a _____

on a rock and a _____

in the water.

6 Unjumble these letters to make list words. Draw a picture for each word.

ibdr _____

upypp _____

gofr _____

aknes _____

ueosm _____

tieknt _____

7 Finish these sentences about list words with your own ideas.
Underline the list words.

A new puppy needs _____.

A kitten likes to play with _____.

A pony is fun because _____.

I would like to have a lizard because _____.

p words

pat	pet	pin	pan	pip
pen	pig	pup	pot	peg

1 Write the **p** words that match the pictures. Then colour the pictures.

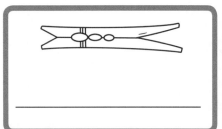  

_____   _____   _____

2 Choose a list word to finish each sentence. Draw a picture about one sentence.

My _____ fish are gold and black.

I like to _____ my dog.

The plant looks good in this _____.

3 Can you find the list words hidden in the box? Write them down.

c	p	a	t	o	e
b	u	s	p	i	p
s	p	o	t	i	p
g	o	p	e	n	m
p	e	g	g	u	n
m	o	p	p	e	t

_____   _____

_____   _____

_____   _____

4 Write the missing vowel in each of these words.

 p____n

 p____g

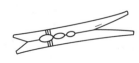 p____g

 p____p

 p____n

5 Find list words to match these patterns.

6 Complete the cartoon with list words and pictures.
Add speech bubbles with your own ideas.

Roxy was my very first _____.	Everyone liked to _____ her.	Now Roxy was a naughty _____.
She opened the pig _____.	The _____ got out.	I still love my _____ Roxy.

7 Imagine you really want a new pet.
Write a letter to Mum or Dad using some list words. Try to persuade them.

Dear _____,

_____

_____

Love from _____

r words

rag	rat	rub	rod	rip
ran	run	rug	ram	rob

1 Write the **r** words that match the pictures. Then colour the pictures.

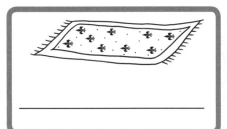  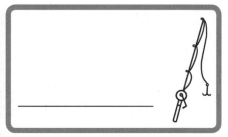

_____ _____ _____

2 Choose a list word to finish each sentence. Draw a picture about one sentence.

He _____ all the way home.

The _____ lives at the farm.

We sat on the picnic _____.

3 Can you find the list words hidden in the box? Write them down.

c	a	r	u	b	m
y	r	o	d	a	b
c	u	p	r	i	p
r	a	n	o	t	e
c	r	o	b	e	e
j	a	r	r	u	n

_____ _____

_____ _____

_____ _____

4 Write the missing vowel in each of these words.

r____t

r____g

r____d

r____g

r____m

34

5 Find and write list words to answer 'What am I?'

I have wool.   I catch fish.   I can wipe.
I have horns.   I have a reel.   Clean with me.

What am I?   What am I?   What am I?

_____   _____   _____

6 Unjumble these letters to make **r** words. Draw pictures to match the words.

dor _____

unr _____

rta _____

obr _____

ugr _____

bur _____

7 Use these list words in sentences of your own.

rat _____

ram _____

rug _____

rip _____

sad	set	sag	sap	sum
sat	sit	sun	sip	sob

1 Write the **s** words that match the pictures. Then colour the pictures.

_____

_____

_____

2 Choose a list word to finish each sentence. Draw a picture about one sentence.

I will _____ my drink.

This is _____ on the tree.

We _____ down and ate our food.

3 Can you find the list words hidden in the box? Write them down.

a	s	e	t	o	p
s	o	b	o	y	s
f	i	x	s	i	t
s	a	d	d	a	m
n	o	s	a	t	e
w	s	i	p	i	e

_____   _____

_____   _____

_____   _____

4 Write the missing vowel in each of these words.

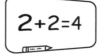
2+2=4

s____m

s____n

s____g

36

5 Find list words to match these patterns.

6 Complete these crossword puzzles with list words.

A   B   C   D

A   Across feeling bad
    Down rested

C   Across hot
    Down add up

B   Across from a tree
    Down cry

D   Across little drink
    Down hang down

7 Make up the start of each sentence. Include a list word in each sentence.

_____ on the end of the bed.

_____ makes plants grow.

_____ in the garden.

_____ a cup of tea.

_____ out of the tree.

_____ my lemonade.

_____ when her toy broke.

t words

tap	tin	tan	tub	tag
tot	top	tip	tug	tab

1 Write the **t** words that match the pictures. Then colour the pictures.

_____

_____

_____

2 Choose a list word to finish each sentence. Draw a picture about one sentence.

This is the hot _____.

Don't _____ the pram over.

The _____ boat led the ship.

3 Can you find the list words hidden in the box? Write them down.

o	u	t	t	a	n
f	e	d	t	a	b
t	a	g	e	g	g
e	a	t	o	p	m
s	t	u	g	u	n
n	o	d	t	o	t

_____ _____

_____ _____

_____ _____

4 Write the missing vowel in each of these words.

t ____ n

t ____ p

t ____ t

t ____ p

t ____ b

38

5 Find and write list words to rhyme with these words.

bag _____   map _____   sip _____   fan _____

pop _____   bug _____   bin _____   pot _____

cot _____   man _____   win _____   rug _____

rip _____   cap _____   rag _____   mop _____

6 Unjumble these letters to make **t** words. Draw pictures to match the words.

ott _____

ant _____

gtu _____

bta _____

gat _____

apt _____

7 Use these list words in sentences of your own.

tub _____

tag _____

tan _____

tot _____

Revision: Winter

a b c d e f g h i j k l m n o p q r s t u v w x y z

1 Put the list words into alphabetical order below. Use the list word when making up a beginning for the sentence next door.

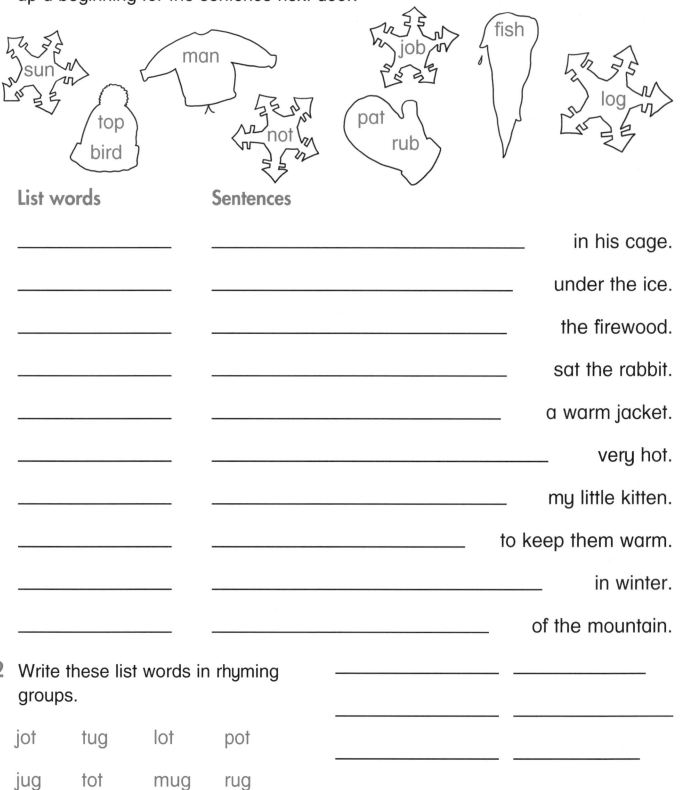

List words   **Sentences**

_____   _____   in his cage.

_____   _____   under the ice.

_____   _____   the firewood.

_____   _____   sat the rabbit.

_____   _____   a warm jacket.

_____   _____   very hot.

_____   _____   my little kitten.

_____   _____   to keep them warm.

_____   _____   in winter.

_____   _____   of the mountain.

2 Write these list words in rhyming groups.

jot   tug   lot   pot

jug   tot   mug   rug

_____   _____

_____   _____

_____   _____

3 Complete this crossword puzzle about pets.

Across
2 sleeps in the sun
4 whistles
6 playful
8 squeaks
9 trots around

Down
1 swims in a tank
3 has a fluffy tail
5 very long
7 barks

4 Use all these list words in a story of your own about winter.

men   ran   map   job   pup   met

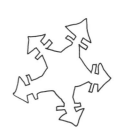

_____

_____

_____

_____

_____

v and **w** words

van	**v**at	**w**eb	**w**ax	**w**et
vet	**w**in	**w**ag	**w**ig	

1 Write the list words that match the pictures. Then colour the pictures.

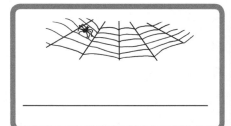

_____

_____

_____

2 Choose a list word to finish each sentence. Draw a picture about one sentence.

My sick dog went to the _____.

Today is _____ and cold.

The _____ made the floor shine.

3 Can you find the list words hidden in the box? Write them down.

w	a	x	c	a	r
g	o	v	a	t	e
v	e	t	i	n	d
w	i	n	i	n	e
u	s	w	a	g	e
w	e	t	r	y	e

_____ _____

_____ _____

_____ _____

4 Write the missing vowel in each of these words.

 v ____ t

 v ____ n

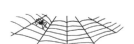 w ____ b

  w ____ g

5 Find list words to match these patterns.

6 Complete the cartoon about a vet with list words and pictures.
Add speech bubbles with your own ideas.

The vet was having a funny day.

A dog's tail had lost its _____.

A spider had fallen from her _____.

A duck got _____.

A rat had fallen in a _____.

The _____ was very busy.

7 Find a list word to match each clue.

a doctor for animals _____

a spider's home _____

this is yellow and candles are made from it _____

not dry _____

43

y and z words

yes	**y**am	**y**ak	**z**ap
yet	**y**ap	**y**um	**z**ip

1 Write the list words that match the pictures. Then colour the pictures.

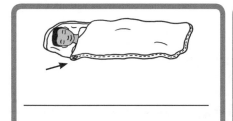

_____

_____

_____

2 Choose a list word to finish each sentence. Draw a picture about one sentence.

Mum said, 'No, not _____.'

The dog likes to _____.

The sleeping bag has a big _____.

3 Can you find the list words hidden in the box? Write them down.

c	y	a	k	a	s
m	y	e	t	e	l
p	e	t	z	a	p
r	o	t	y	e	s
b	u	y	u	m	d
y	a	p	o	l	d

_____ _____

_____ _____

_____ _____

4 Put a circle around each correct word in brackets.

I have a (yes, zip) in my dress.

You can eat a (yam, yet).

Claire saw the ice-cream and said ('Yap', 'Yum').

5 Find list words to match these patterns.

6 Unjumble these letters to make **y** and **z** words. Draw pictures to match the words.

ayp _____

pza _____

sey _____

may _____

zpi _____

7 Use these list words in sentences of your own.

yum _____

zip _____

yet _____

yes _____

sh words

di**sh**	**sh**ed	**sh**op	**sh**ut	ca**sh**
da**sh**	**sh**ip	**sh**ot	wi**sh**	ra**sh**

1 Write the **sh** words that match the pictures. Then colour the pictures.

_____

_____

_____

2 Choose a list word to finish each sentence. Draw a picture about one sentence.

The garden tools are in the _____.

I like to go to the toy _____.

The farmer _____ the fox.

3 Can you find the list words hidden in the box? Write them down.

w	a	s	h	o	t
r	a	s	h	o	e
s	h	u	t	e	n
s	w	i	s	h	e
h	i	s	h	e	d
r	c	a	s	h	e

_____ _____

_____ _____

_____ _____

4 Write the missing vowel in each of these words.

sh____p

sh____p

sh____d

d____sh

d____sh

5 Find list words to match these patterns.

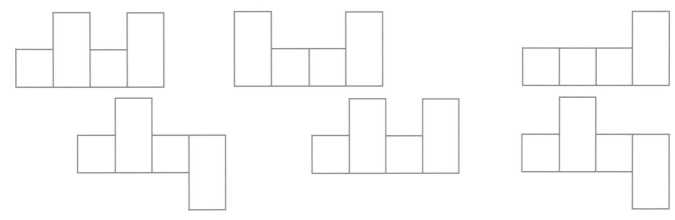

6 Here is an acrostic poem for the list word dash. Make up acrostic poems of your own for list words. Draw a picture for each.

down the street _____ _____

at top speed _____ _____

sprint so fast _____ _____

hurry! hurry! _____ _____

7 Unjumble these sentences containing list words. Underline the list words. Draw a picture for each.

ship The to Australia. sailed
_____
_____

was wish I shop the shut. not that
_____
_____

–ll words

bell	fell	hill	tell	will
doll	fill	sell	well	pill

1 Write the **ll** words that match the pictures. Then colour the pictures.

_____

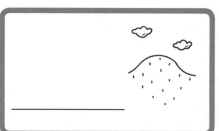

_____

_____

2 Choose a list word to finish each sentence. Draw a picture about one sentence.

Jack _____ down the hill.

Dad will _____ us a story.

I will _____ my cup with milk.

3 Can you find the list words hidden in the box? Write them down.

e	f	i	l	l	y
t	e	l	l	e	t
s	w	e	l	l	m
h	i	s	e	l	l
w	i	l	l	o	g
e	f	e	l	l	s

_____ _____

_____ _____

_____ _____

4 Write the missing vowel in each of these words.

d ____ ll

p ____ ll

b ____ ll

h ____ ll

w ____ ll

5 a b c d e f g h i j k l m n o p q r s t u v w x y z

Put these list words into alphabetical order and draw a picture for each.

well   tell   sell   bell   fell

_____	_____	_____	_____	_____

6 Unjumble these letters to make **ll** words. Draw pictures to match the words.

tlle _____

hlli _____

ldol _____

lsel _____

plil _____

blel _____

7 Write a letter to your grandmother, using as many of the list words as you can.

_____

_____

_____

_____

Theme words: Days

Sunday	Tuesday	Thursday	Saturday	today
Monday	Wednesday	Friday	yesterday	tomorrow

1 Write three list words in the spaces and draw a picture for each.

_____	_____	_____

2 Choose a list word to finish each sentence.

We start the school week on _____.

We end the school week on _____.

I am very happy _____.

3 Can you find six list words hidden in the box? Write them down.

a	S	u	n	d	a	y	S
u	T	u	e	s	d	a	y
t	o	d	a	y	W	o	v
n	F	r	i	d	a	y	g
T	h	u	r	s	d	a	y
e	M	o	n	d	a	y	k

_____ _____

_____ _____

_____ _____

4 Write in the missing capital letter for each of these list words.

____ ednesday

____ hursday

____ aturday

____ riday

____ onday

5 Find small words in these list words.

Sunday _____ _____ _____   tomorrow _____ _____ _____

Saturday _____ _____ _____   today _____ _____ _____

yesterday _____ _____ _____   Monday _____ _____ _____

6 What list word am I? Draw about your favourite day.

I have the vowels **i** and **a**.   _____

I have the vowels **a**, **u** and **a**.   _____

I have three **o** vowels.   _____

My vowels are **u**, **e** and **a**.   _____

I have two **e** vowels and an **a**.   _____

My vowels are **o** and **a**.   _____

7 Unjumble these sentences containing list words. Underline the list words.

played I On Saturday with friend. my tennis

_____.

borrowed three on I from story library Monday. books the

_____.

Wednesday like I we do art because school. at day the it is

_____.

am a birthday. Thursday Next I having party my for

_____.

had Yesterday my cat three kittens. little

_____.

ch words

chin	chip	chat	rich	much
chop	chap	chum	such	

1 Write the **ch** words that match the pictures. Then colour the pictures.

 _____

 _____

 _____

2 Choose a list word to finish each sentence. Draw a picture about one sentence.

We ran _____ a long way.

He ate too _____ cake.

My _____ came to play with me.

3 Can you find the list words hidden in the box? Write them down.

c	h	a	t	e	s
s	u	c	h	i	m
c	r	i	c	h	e
e	a	c	h	a	p
s	m	u	c	h	y
o	u	c	h	u	m

_____ _____

_____ _____

_____ _____

4 Write the missing vowel in each of these words.

ch ____ p

ch ____ p

ch ____ p

ch ____ n

5 Find list words to match these patterns.

6 Unjumble these letters to make **ch** words. Draw pictures to match the words.

mhuc _____

hcta _____

hric _____

phoc _____

hucs _____

chni _____

7 Use these list words in sentences of your own.

rich _____

chat _____

chop _____

much _____

ee words

feed	see	tree	weed	deep
feet	sheep	seed	bee	keep

1 Write the **ee** words that match the pictures. Then colour the pictures.

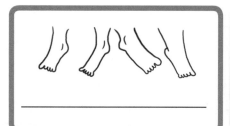

_____

_____

_____

2 Choose a list word to finish each sentence. Draw a picture about one sentence.

That _____ can sting.

I went to _____ my nanna.

I will plant this little _____ .

3 Can you find the list words hidden in the box? Write them down.

s	e	e	d	r	y
g	e	k	e	e	p
a	s	h	e	e	p
w	e	e	d	u	g
w	i	f	e	e	d
d	e	e	p	e	a

_____ _____

_____ _____

_____ _____

4 Write the missing vowels in each of these words.

 b ____ ____

 sh ____ ____ p

 f ____ ____ t

 s ____ ____ d

 tr ____ ____

54

5 Find list words to match these patterns.

6 Unjumble these letters to make **ee** words. Draw pictures to match the words.

efed _____

ekep _____

ebe _____

etre _____

sehep _____

teef _____

7 Write two list words to rhyme with each word below.

weed _____   _____

see _____   _____

deep _____   _____

55

–ng words

ring	sing	king	wing	swing
long	song	strong	belong	gong

1 Write the **ng** words that match the pictures. Then colour the pictures.

_____

_____

_____

2 Choose and write list words to finish the sentences. Draw a picture about one sentence.

I like to _____ my favourite _____.

Ants are very _____ for their size.

I go up high on my _____.

3 Can you find the list words hidden in the box? Write them down.

a	w	i	n	g	t
s	i	n	g	m	s
s	e	l	o	n	g
n	s	w	i	n	g
b	e	l	o	n	g
e	g	o	n	g	r

_____ _____

_____ _____

_____ _____

4 Write the missing vowels in each of these words.

b ___ l ___ ng

r ___ ng

l ___ ng

sw ___ ng

str ___ ng

k ___ ng

5 Find and write list words to answer 'What am I?'

I am not short.
I rhyme with song.

What am I?

_____

I can lift.
I have muscles.

What am I?

_____

I go up and down.
I have a seat.

What am I?

_____

6 Complete the crossword puzzles with list words. Then make up two puzzles of your own below with list words for answers. Let a friend solve your puzzles.

Across **not short**
Down **a tune**

Across **part of the group**
Down **makes a loud noise**

7 Finish these sentences containing list words with your own ideas.

If I was king I would_____.

I sometimes ring _____.

I belong to_____.

A long time ago _____.

th words

the	them	this	thud	with
that	then	thin	than	maths

1 Write the **th** words that match the pictures. Then colour the pictures.

_____

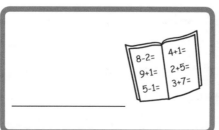

_____

_____

2 Choose a list word to finish each sentence. Draw a picture about one sentence.

Tell _____ to come in.

He fell with a _____.

I will sit _____ mum and dad.

3 Can you find the list words hidden in the box? Write them down.

l	o	t	h	e	m
t	h	i	s	a	y
i	t	h	e	s	a
t	o	w	i	t	h
t	h	e	n	u	r
i	w	t	h	a	t

_____   _____

_____   _____

_____   _____

4 Put a circle around each correct word in brackets.

(That, Maths) is my house.

Do you like (this, than) dress?

In (thin, the) pond was a fish.

5 a b c d e f g h i j k l m n o p q r s t u v w x y z

Put these list words into alphabetical order and draw a picture for each.

than   that   thud   maths   them

_____	_____	_____	_____	_____

6 Find small words in each of these list words.

the   _____   maths _____ _____ _____

them _____ _____ _____   thin   _____ _____

then _____ _____ _____   this   _____ _____ _____

that _____ _____ _____   with   _____ _____ _____

7 Unjumble these sentences containing list words. Underline the **th** words.

grandfather My very thin. is tall and

_____.

nine year brother My old very maths. is good at

_____.

mother on went baby My the with bus sister. my

_____.

day Saturday Monday. it Sunday, The after is and then comes

_____.

is my This that aunt and is uncle. my

_____.

59

Revision: Spring

a b c d e f g h i j k l m n o p q r s t u v w x y z

1 Put the list words into alphabetical order below. Use the list word when making up a beginning for the sentence next door.

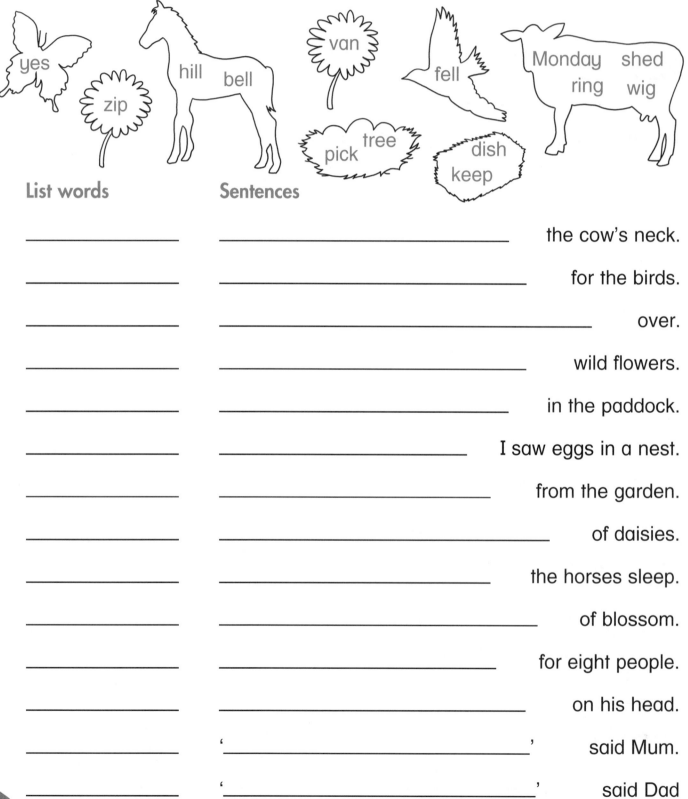

List words   **Sentences**

_____   _____   the cow's neck.

_____   _____   for the birds.

_____   _____   over.

_____   _____   wild flowers.

_____   _____   in the paddock.

_____   _____   I saw eggs in a nest.

_____   _____   from the garden.

_____   _____   of daisies.

_____   _____   the horses sleep.

_____   _____   of blossom.

_____   _____   for eight people.

_____   _____   on his head.

_____   '_____' said Mum.

_____   '_____' said Dad

60

2 Complete this crossword puzzle about days.

Across

1 after today
3 after Tuesday
5 now
8 after Thursday
9 a day of rest
10 after Monday

Down

2 the school week begins
4 part of the weekend
6 before today
7 before Friday

3 Use all these list words in a story of your own about spring.

seed   deep   much   sing   song   see

_____

_____

_____

_____

61

–ck words

back	neck	pick	sick	lick
duck	pack	rock	kick	sock

1 Write the **ck** words that match the pictures. Then colour the pictures.

_____

_____

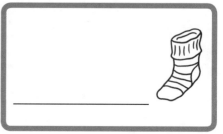

_____

2 Choose a list word to finish each sentence. Draw a picture about one sentence.

I will _____ my bag.

Help me to _____ up the toys.

We swam _____ to the rocks.

3 Can you find the list words hidden in the box? Write them down.

a	p	i	c	k	b
s	o	c	k	e	y
i	l	l	i	c	k
m	a	d	u	c	k
s	i	c	k	o	f
c	r	o	c	k	n

_____ _____

_____ _____

_____ _____

4 Write the missing vowel in each of these words.

n____ck

k____ck

s____ck

d____ck

r____ck

5 Find and write list words to answer 'What am I?'

I keep feet warm.   I have cards.   I feel ill.
I have a pair.   Play with me.   I stay in bed.

What am I?   What am I?   What am I?

_____   _____   _____

6 Here is an acrostic poem for the list word sock. Make up acrostic poems of
your own for list words. Draw pictures.

soft   _____   _____

on my foot   _____   _____

cotton or woollen   _____   _____

keeps me warm   _____   _____

7 Unjumble these sentences containing list words. Underline the **ck** words.

cat My Oscar to likes his fur. lick

_____.

ran the after My Jess dog duck.

_____.

play on in We the yard. back swing the

_____.

–nd words

band	land	sand	wind	bend
hand	pond	send	mend	end

1 Write the **nd** words that match the pictures. Then colour the pictures.

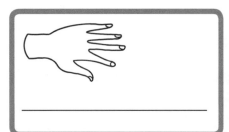
_____

_____

_____

2 Choose a list word to finish each sentence. Draw a picture about one sentence.

The _____ will play and we will march.

I will _____ a letter to you.

He likes to play in the _____ pit.

3 Can you find the list words hidden in the box? Write them down.

s	b	a	n	d	y
y	e	s	e	n	d
s	g	e	n	d	e
l	a	n	d	e	n
k	m	e	n	d	s
g	a	s	a	n	d

_____ _____

_____ _____

_____ _____

4 Write the missing vowel in each of these words.

b ____ nd

p ____ nd

s ____ nd

64

5 Find list words to match these patterns.

6 Unjumble these letters to make **nd** words. Draw pictures to match the words.

bnde _____

snde _____

nde _____

dnah _____

pnod _____

niwd _____

7 Find list words to answer 'What am I?'

My people play musical instruments. What am I? _____

I am found at the beach. What am I? _____

I blow the leaves around. What am I? _____

I have four fingers and a thumb. What am I? _____

–st words

best	must	rest	vest	lost
dust	nest	west	test	cost

1 Write the **st** words that match the pictures. Then colour the pictures.

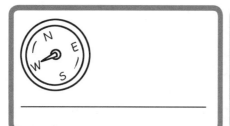

_____

_____

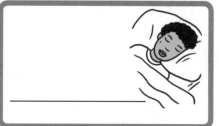

_____

2 Choose a list word to finish each sentence. Draw a picture about one sentence.

This is my _____ dress.

How much did that book _____?

I have _____ my ring.

3 Can you find the list words hidden in the box? Write them down.

e	v	e	s	t	y
b	e	s	t	o	e
p	a	c	o	s	t
e	m	u	s	t	p
c	l	o	s	t	e
t	e	s	t	e	n

_____   _____

_____   _____

_____   _____

4 Put a circle around each correct word in brackets.

The egg was in the (lost, nest).

I need a (rest, west).

There is (dust, must) on that old book.

5 a b c d e f g h i j k l m n o p q r s t u v w x y z

Put these list words into alphabetical order and draw a picture for each.

cost   west   dust   vest   best

_____	_____	_____	_____	_____

6 Here is an acrostic poem for the list word lost. Choose any list words and make up acrostic poems of your own. Draw a picture for each.

lonely   _____   _____

on my own   _____   _____

scared   _____   _____

take me home   _____   _____

7 Choose a list word to answer 'What am I?'

I see if you can do something. What am I? _____

I am better than all the others. What am I? _____

I am a piece of clothing. What am I? _____

Birds make me out of twigs. What am I? _____

When you are tired you need me. What am I? _____

–mp words

jump	pump	limp	camp	dump
lump	ramp	romp	lamp	bump

1 Write the **mp** words that match the pictures. Then colour the pictures.

_____

_____

_____

2 Choose a list word to finish each sentence. Draw a picture about one sentence.

I like to run, skip and _____.

My dog likes to _____ at the beach.

We walked up the _____ onto the ship.

3 Can you find the list words hidden in the box? Write them down.

c	l	u	m	p	s
r	o	m	p	e	r
a	b	l	i	m	p
j	u	m	p	e	r
c	a	r	a	m	p
d	u	m	p	i	g

_____   _____

_____   _____

_____   _____

4 Write the missing vowel in each of these words.

r____mp

l____mp

l____mp

5 Find list words to match these patterns.

6 Complete the cartoon using list words and pictures.
Add speech bubbles with your own ideas.

There was trouble at the _____.	My _____ blew out in the dark.	I heard a _____ in the night.
I fell down a big _____.	I got a _____ on my head.	I wanted to _____ on the bus home.

7 Find a list word to match each clue.

a swelling _____

a place where people live in tents or huts _____

something that gives light _____

walk with a sore foot _____

Theme words: Colours

red	green	blue	yellow	purple
orange	white	black	brown	pink

1 Write the list words that match the pictures. Then colour the pictures.

_____

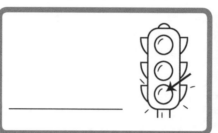

_____

_____

2 Choose list words to finish each sentence. Draw a picture about one sentence.

Grapes can be _____ and _____ .

Hair can be _____, _____, _____,

_____, _____ and _____.

3 Can you find the list words hidden in the box? Write them down.

a	p	u	r	p	l	e	t
p	i	n	k	b	r	e	d
o	o	g	r	e	e	n	v
b	l	u	e	d	m	a	g
g	h	u	w	h	i	t	e
e	x	o	r	a	n	g	e

_____

_____

_____

_____

_____

_____

_____

4 Write down the list words that have an **e** in them. _____

_____ _____ _____

_____ _____ _____

5 Find small words in these list words.

yellow _____ _____   black _____ _____

brown _____ _____ _____   white _____ _____ _____

pink _____ _____ _____ _____

orange _____ _____ _____ _____ _____

6 What list word am I? Draw about your favourite colour.

I have the vowels o, a and e. _____

I only have the vowel i.   _____

I only have the vowel o.   _____

My vowels are i and e.   _____

I have two e vowels.   _____

My vowels are u and e.   _____

7 Unjumble these sentences containing list words. Underline the list words.

of the Green the colours and blue sea. are

_____.

Yellow and stars. moon is the sun, colour of the

_____.

mountains far Purple is the the colour away. of

_____.

stop light. the colour of Red is the

_____.

71

–y (= 'i') words

by	dry	my	try	shy
cry	fly	sky	sty	fry

1 Write the y words that match the pictures. Then colour the pictures.

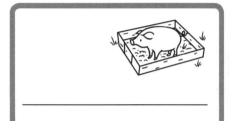

_____

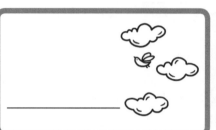

_____

_____

2 Choose a list word to finish each sentence. Draw a picture about one sentence.

My little sister is a bit _____.

Wind and sun will _____ the washing.

You must _____ to do your best.

3 Can you find the list words hidden in the box? Write them down.

a	n	d	r	y	d
r	t	r	y	e	w
b	y	j	a	m	n
i	s	m	y	h	o
i	c	r	y	a	s
l	i	d	s	h	y

_____ _____

_____ _____

_____ _____

4 Put a circle around each correct word in brackets.

A pig lives in a (shy, sty).

Lots of clouds were in the

(sky, fry).

Scott started to (by, cry).

5 a b c d e f g h i j k l m n o p q r s t u v w x y z

Put these list words into alphabetical order and draw a picture for each.

try   sky   cry   fly   dry

6 Unjumble these letters to make **y** words. Draw pictures to match the words.

yrt _____

fyr _____

syt _____

hsy _____

ydr _____

lyf _____

7 Use these list words in sentences of your own.

my _____

cry _____

sty _____

73

all words

| all | call | small | wall | stall |
| ball | fall | tall | hall | |

1 Write the **all** words that match the pictures. Then colour the pictures.

_____

_____

_____

2 Choose a list word to finish each sentence. Draw a picture about one sentence.

We _____ went to the party.

That tree is too _____ for our garden.

May I have a _____ drink please?

3 Can you find the list words hidden in the box? Write them down.

o	h	a	l	l	i
s	t	a	l	l	r
a	l	l	e	g	g
u	w	a	l	l	r
g	o	c	a	l	l
i	s	m	a	l	l

_____ _____

_____ _____

_____ _____

4 Put a circle around each correct word in the brackets.

Jan threw the (wall, ball).

The horse was in the (small, stall).

Humpty Dumpty sat on a

(wall, hall).

5 Find list words to match these patterns.

6 Unjumble these letters to make **all** words. Draw pictures to match the words.

blla _____

tslla _____

lcal _____

lal _____

mslla _____

tlla _____

7 Find list words to answer 'What am I?'

I am cosy and horses stay in me. What am I? _____

I am up high like a tree. What am I? _____

I am little like a baby. What am I? _____

I am long and lead to rooms. What am I? _____

Essential words 1

about	were	down	have	from	to
people	are	school	like	night	too
after	because	what	morning	there	of
when	saw	her	came	their	off

1 Write the list words that match the pictures. Then colour the pictures.

_____

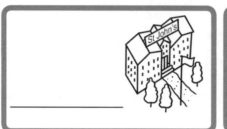

_____

_____

2 Choose a list word to finish each sentence. Draw about one sentence.

I got a letter _____ my grandmother this morning.

I like chocolate _____ it is yummy.

I read _____ animals in my zoo book.

3 Can you find the list words hidden in the box? Write them down.

t	a	f	t	e	r
p	e	o	p	l	e
w	h	e	n	f	f
t	o	a	a	r	e
g	l	i	k	e	w
t	o	o	d	o	f

_____ _____

_____ _____

_____ _____

_____ _____

4 Write in the first letter for each of these list words.

__ orning   __ ff   __ here   __ aw

__ own   __ er   __ hat   __ rom

__ ave   __ ame   __ ere   __ heir

5 a b c d e f g h i j k l m n o p q r s t u v w x y z

Put these list words into alphabetical order and draw a picture for each.

people   school   down   like   her

_____	_____	_____	_____	_____

6 Find small words in these list words.

because   _____ _____ _____ _____   too   _____

down   _____ _____   off   _____

what   _____ _____ _____   morning   _____ _____

their   _____ _____ _____ _____   were   _____

there   _____ _____ _____   when   _____ _____

7 Unjumble these sentences containing list words. Underline the list words.

grandfather me from came My school. to up pick

_____.

sister My down the ran after street me.

_____.

do want to on What you Monday? do

_____?

cousins pony. their My are taking me to see

_____.

77

Essential words 2

very	just	little	she	play	out
went	for	our	soon	could	where
day	home	over	you	said	they
going	some	time	water	good	was

1 Write the list words that match the pictures. Then colour the pictures.

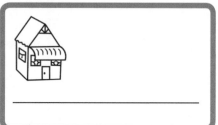

2 Choose a list word to finish each sentence. Draw about one sentence.

David and Carmel _____ in the snow.

'Look at the little penguins!' _____ Sam.

We are _____ on a holiday when it is summer.

3 Can you find the list words hidden in the box? Write them down.

t	c	o	u	l	d
a	n	s	f	o	r
s	o	o	n	e	e
w	a	t	e	r	f
w	a	s	s	l	s
y	o	u	d	a	t

_____ _____

_____ _____

_____ _____

4 Write in the first letter for each of these list words.

____ aid   ____ ut

____ ome   ____ hey

____ ur   ____ ver

78

5 a b c d e f g h i j k l m n o p q r s t u v w x y z

Put these list words into alphabetical order and draw a picture for each.

day   over   little   she   water

_____	_____	_____	_____	_____

6 Find small words in each of these list words.

water   _____ _____   good   _____ _____

where   _____ _____ _____   going   _____ _____

they   _____ _____ _____   soon   _____ _____

little   _____ _____ _____   time   _____ _____

some   _____ _____   play   _____ _____

she   _____ went   _____

7 Unjumble these sentences containing list words. Underline the list words.

home Mother. is trees,' the bird's little in said 'The

_____.

the We over went blue play near water. to

_____.

pet out the sunshine. snake Our in was

_____.

Revision: Summer

a b c d e f g h i j k l m n o p q r s t u v w x y z

1 Put the list words into alphabetical order below.
Use the list word when making up a beginning for the sentence next door.

orange

when   duck

their

lick

camp   nest   ball   green

fly

kick   vest

end   said

List words   **Sentences**

_____   _____   on the sand.

_____   _____   summer holiday.

_____   _____   at the river

_____   _____   very tired.

_____   _____   into the trees.

_____   _____   summertime.

_____   '_____,'   yelled my brother.

_____   _____   before it melts.

_____   _____   flew the birds.

_____   _____   fruit salad.

_____   _____, 'Turn on the fan please.'

_____   _____   for a barbecue.

_____   _____   under my jacket.

_____   _____   we stay up later.

2 Complete this crossword puzzle about colours.

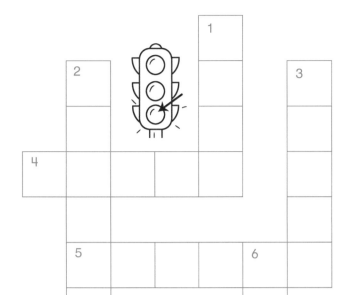

Across

4 __ as night
5 a fruit colour
8 says stop
9 tree trunks
10 clear sky

Down

1 mix red and white
2 sunny
3 snowy
6 grass is __
7 mix red and blue

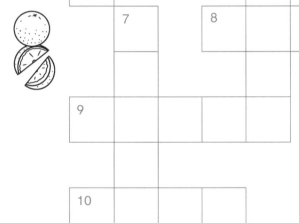

3 Use all these list words in a story of your own about summer.

their   there   to   too   of   off

_____

_____

_____

_____

4 Use the words below to label this break-up scene. Then colour in the picture.

jump   ball   wall   play   nest

neck   ramp   hand   water   sock

These groups can be extended with the class and introduced throughout the year as the need arises. Teachers can devise activities for the blends similar to those provided in the book.

Examples of initial blends

sl	sp	sw	cl	pl	dr	gr
slap	spot	swim	clam	play	drum	grab
slim	spin	sweep	clap	plus	drop	grub
slam	spill	sweet	club	plant	drink	grin
sm	sc	sn	fl	br	pr	fr
small	scab	snap	flag	brick	pram	frog
smack	scar	snip	flat	brush	print	fry
smash	school	snack	fly	bran	pray	fresh
st	sk	bl	gl	cr	tr	tw
stop	skin	black	glad	crab	tram	twin
star	skip	blond	glum	crash	trap	twig
sty	sky	blob	glitter	cry	trip	twenty

Examples of final blends

st	nd	lt	ct	ang	ung
rest	stand	melt	act	sang	sung
lost	bend	felt	fact	hang	stung
dust	pond	belt	strict	rang	lung
mp	ft	nk	lp	ing	lf
lamp	left	ink	help	wing	elf
stamp	soft	think	yelp	king	golf
jump	gift	pink	kelp	swing	shelf
nt	sk	lk	pt	ong	ld
ant	desk	milk	kept	long	held
tent	risk	silk	slept	song	told
hunt	mask	sulk	crept	strong	cold

List words

b
bad
bag
bat
bed
big
bit
box
bun
bus
but

c
can
cap
cat
cot
cup
cut
cab
cub

d
dad
did
dig
dog
dug
dim
dam
dab
den
dot

Numbers
one
two

three
four
five
six
seven
eight
nine
ten

f
fat
fed
fix
fox
fun
fan
fig
fin
fit
fog

g
get
got
gum
gun
gap
god
gas
gut

h
has
hat
hen
hid
hit

him
his
hop
hot
hut

Family
mother
father
sister
brother
grandmother
grandfather
aunt
uncle
cousin
baby

j
jam
jug
jig
job
jog
jet
jab
jot

l
leg
let
lit
log
lot
lid
lip
led

lad
lap

m
man
mat
men
met
mud
mop
map
mix
mug
mum

n
net
not
nut
nap
nip
nod
nag
nun

Pets
puppy
kitten
mouse
bird
pony
rabbit
frog
lizard
fish
snake

p
pat
pen
pet
pig
pin
pup
pan
pot
pip
peg

r
rag
ran
rat
run
rub
rug
rod
ram
rip
rob

s
sad
sat
set
sit
sag
sun
sap
sip
sum
sob

t
tap
tot
tin
top
tan
tip
tub
tug
tag
tab

v and w
van
vet
vat
win
web
wag
wax
wig
wet

y and z
yes
yet
yam
yap
yak
yum
zap
zip

sh
dish
dash
shed

ship
shop
shot
shut
wish
cash
rash

–ll
bell
doll
fell
fill
hill
sell
tell
well
will
pill

Days
Sunday
Monday
Tuesday
Wednesday
Thursday
Friday
Saturday
yesterday
today
tomorrow

ch
chin
chop
chip
chap
chat
chum
rich

such
much

ee
feed
feet
see
sheep
tree
seed
weed
bee
deep
keep

–ng
ring
long
sing
song
king
strong
wing
belong
swing
gong

th
the
that
them
then
this
thin
thud
than
with
maths

–ck
back
duck
neck
pack
pick
rock
sick
kick
lick
sock

–nd
band
hand
land
pond
sand
send
wind
mend
bend
end

–st
best
dust
must
nest
rest
west
vest
test
lost
cost

–mp
jump
lump
pump
ramp
limp
romp
camp
lamp
dump
bump

Colours
red
orange
green
white
blue
black
yellow
brown
purple
pink

–y (= 'i')
by
cry
dry
fly
my
sky
try
sty
shy
fry

all
all
ball
call
fall
small
tall
wall
hall
stall

**Essential
words 1**
about
down
like
from
people
school
morning
because
after
what
there
their
her
saw
of
to
are
too
off
when
were
night
have
came

**Essential
words 2**
very
time
said
went
just
soon
good
day
for
you
out
going
little
water
where
our
she
home
over
play
they
some
could
was

Dictation sentences

Words in italics are new list words for the week. Words in bold are words previously introduced; these are included as revision. Punctuation includes the capital letter, full stop, comma and question mark.

b

The *big bun* is in the *box*.

c

The **bad** *cat can* jump in the *cot*.

d

The *dog* **can** see the **cub** in the *dim den*.

Numbers

My **dog** is *seven* and my **cat** is *eight*.

f

In the *fog*, the *fat fox fed* on **three bats**.

g

The *gum* trees at the **dam** *got* very **big**.

h

Dad *hid* **four** eggs in a **box** under *his* **fig** tree.

Family

My *grandmother* **has one** *brother* and **one** *sister*.

j

My **cousin** and I had **six** *jam* **buns** on the **big** *jet*.

l

The **fit dog** *led* the *lad* to **his grandfather** at the *log* **hut**.

m

My *mum* **has** to *mop* up the *mud* on the *mat*.

n

The **two baby** twins had a *nap* under the *net* on the **cot**.

Pets

I have **five** *fish* and my **sister has** a pet *mouse* and a *rabbit* that **can hop**.

p

My **uncle** and **aunt fed** the **nine fat** *pigs* in the *pig pen*.

r

The **kitten** *ran* to the *rug* to **get** the **big** *rat*.

s

The **mother lizard** *set* out to *sit* in the **hot** *sun*.

t

The *tot* and **his two brothers** had **fun** in the *tub*.

v and w

The *vet* **has** the **sad, pet snake** in **his** *van*.

y and z

Has grandfather got jam on **his big,** **fat** *yam? Yes.*

sh

My **big brother has** *cash* for a **puppy** and a *dish* from the **pet** *shop.*

–ll

Tell my **grandmother** my *doll fell* in the *well* on the *hill.*

Days

I go on the **bus** on *Monday, Tuesday, Wednesday, Thursday* and *Friday.*

ch

The *chap* **will** *chop* up **ten logs today** and **ten logs tomorrow**.

ee

Grandfather will *feed* the *sheep* and *see* to the *bees.*

–ng

Will the *king* on the *swing sing* a *long song?*

th

That thin **chap** *with* a black **hat** is my **father.**

–ck

The *sick duck* on **the** *rock* **has** a **bad** *back* and *neck.*

–nd

The strong *wind* **will** *send sand* into **the** *pond.*

–st

Yesterday the bird *lost* her *nest* from **the tree**.

–mp

Can a **baby run, hop, jog**, *jump* and *romp*?

Colours

My **best vest** is *orange, blue, yellow, green, purple* and *white.*

y (= 'i')

Grandmother and I **will** *try* to **see the black birds** *fly by* in **the red** *sky.*

all

The *small* **black** and **white pony** in **the** *stall* **can see** *all* **the sheep.**

Essential words 1

What is *there to* do on **Saturday** *morning after* I **get** up?

Essential words 2

Could you play over at **my** *home just* **after school today?**

My words

Aa

_____
_____
_____
_____

Bb

_____
_____
_____
_____

Cc

_____
_____
_____
_____

Dd

_____
_____
_____
_____

Ee

_____
_____
_____
_____

Ff

_____
_____
_____
_____

Gg

Hh

Ii

Jj

Kk

Ll

Mm

Nn

Oo

Pp

Qq

Rr

Ss

Tt

Uu

Vv

Ww

Xx Yy Zz

Progress record sheet

Unit		Date completed	Comments
Unit 1	Revision of single sounds		
Unit 2	**b** words		
Unit 3	**c** words		
Unit 4	**d** words		
Unit 5	Theme words: Numbers		
Unit 6	**f** words		
Unit 7	**g** words		
Unit 8	**h** words		
Unit 9	Theme words: Family		
Unit 10	Revision: Autumn		
Unit 11	**j** words		
Unit 12	**l** words		
Unit 13	**m** words		
Unit 14	**n** words		
Unit 15	Theme words: Pets		
Unit 16	**p** words		
Unit 17	**r** words		
Unit 18	**s** words		
Unit 19	**t** words		
Unit 20	Revision: Winter		
Unit 21	**v** and **w** words		
Unit 22	**y** and **z** words		
Unit 23	**sh** words		
Unit 24	**–ll** words		
Unit 25	Theme words: Days		
Unit 26	**ch** words		
Unit 27	**ee** words		
Unit 28	**–ng** words		
Unit 29	**th** words		
Unit 30	Revision: Spring		
Unit 31	**–ck** words		
Unit 32	**–nd** words		
Unit 33	**–st** words		
Unit 34	**–mp** words		
Unit 35	Theme words: Colours		
Unit 36	**–y** (= 'i') words		
Unit 37	**all** words		
Unit 38	Essential words 1		
Unit 39	Essential words 2		
Unit 40	Revision: Summer		